WATCH THEM
•••••••
GROW!

The Life Cycle of a
MAPLE TREE

Gale George

PowerKiDS
press.

New York

Published in 2016 by The Rosen Publishing Group, Inc.
29 East 21st Street, New York, NY 10010

First Edition

Editor: Caitie McAneney
Book Design: Reann Nye

Photo Credits: Cover marinatakano/Shutterstock.com; pp. 5, 23 (tree) rsooll/Shutterstock.com; pp. 6, 23 (seed) Kathy Clark/Shutterstock.com; p. 9 Peter Cade/The Image Bank/Getty Images; p. 10 SvitDen/Shutterstock.com; p. 13 Tanchic/Shutterstock.com; pp. 15 (roots and stem), 24 (root) © istockphoto.com/saje; pp. 15 (background), 24 (soil) ifong/Shutterstock.com; p. 16 Denis and Yulia Pogostins/Shutterstock.com; pp. 19, 23 (sprout), 24 (stem) Ina Raschke/Shutterstock.com; pp. 20, 23 (sapling) Anatoly Vlasov/Shutterstock.com.

Library of Congress Cataloging-in-Publication Data

George, Gale, author.
The life cycle of a maple tree / Gale George.
    pages cm. — (Watch them grow!)
Includes bibliographical references and index.
ISBN 978-1-4994-0677-1 (pbk.)
ISBN 978-1-4994-0842-3 (6 pack)
ISBN 978-1-4994-0679-5 (library binding)
1. Maple—Juvenile literature. 2. Maple—Life cycles—Juvenile literature. I. Title. II. Series: Watch them grow!
QK495.A17G46 2015
583'.78—dc23
                          2014048539

Manufactured in the United States of America

CPSIA Compliance Information: Batch #WS15PK: For Further Information contact Rosen Publishing, New York, New York at 1-800-237-9932

Contents

A maple tree changes as it grows. The changes make up the tree's life cycle.

Maple trees drop seeds. Some are carried away by wind and animals.

A seed holds a baby plant and a little food for the plant to grow. A maple seed has wings to help it fly.

9

A maple seed needs water and healthy **soil** to grow.

The baby plant breaks out of the seed. Now, it's a sprout.

13

The sprout's **roots** grow down into the soil. The **stem** grows upward to find sunlight.

stem

roots

15

Next, leaves grow on the sprout. They help the sprout make food.

The maple sprout grows until it's a sapling. Its stem grows harder.

stem →

A sapling looks like a small tree.
It grows into an adult tree.

An adult tree can drop its own seeds. The maple tree life cycle starts again!

Life Cycle of a Maple Tree

Words to Know

root

soil

stem

Index

Websites

Due to the changing nature of Internet links, PowerKids Press has developed an online list of websites related to the subject of this book. This site is updated regularly. Please use this link to access the list: www.powerkidslinks.com/wtg/mapl